9/09

PAWPAWSAURUS
and Other Armored Dinosaurs
by Dougal Dixon

illustrated by
Steve Weston and James Field

PICTURE WINDOW BOOKS
Minneapolis, Minnesota

Picture Window Books
5115 Excelsior Boulevard
Suite 232
Minneapolis, MN 55416
877-845-8392
www.picturewindowbooks.com

Printed in the United States of America.

Library of Congress Cataloging-in-Publication Data
Dixon, Dougal.
Pawpawsaurus and other armored dinosaurs / by
Dougal Dixon ; illustrated by Steve Weston &
James Field.
p. cm. — (Dinosaur find)
Includes index.
ISBN-13: 978-1-4048-4017-1 (library binding)
1. Pawpawsaurus—Juvenile literature.
2. Ornithischia—Juvenile literature. I. Weston, Steve,
ill. II. Field, James, ill. III. Title.
QE862.O65D595 2008
567.915—dc22   2007040925

Acknowledgments
This book was produced for Picture Window Books
by Bender Richardson White, U.K.

Illustrations by James Field (pages 4–5, 9, 13, 15, 21)
and Steve Weston (pages 7, 11, 17, 19). Diagrams
by Stefan Chabluk.

Photographs: i-stockphotos pages 8 (Cliff Parnell),
10 (EcoPic/Nico Smit), 12 (Keith Livingston), 14
(Nancy Nehring), 16 (Greg Brzezinski), 18 (Steven
Allan); bigstock photos 6 (Gary Unwin); Frank Lane
Photo Agency 20 (Sylvestris Fotoservice).

Consultant: John Stidworthy, Scientific Fellow of
the Zoological Society, London, and former
Lecturer in the Education Department, Natural
History Museum, London.

Types of dinosaurs

In this book, a red shape at the top of a left-hand page shows the animal was a meat-eater. A green shape shows it was a plant-eater.

Just how big—or small—were they?

Dinosaurs were many different sizes. We have compared their size to one of the following:

Chicken
2 feet (60 centimeters) tall
Weight 6 pounds (2.7 kilograms)

Adult person
6 feet (1.8 meters) tall
Weight 170 pounds (76.5 kg)

Elephant
10 feet (3 m) tall
Weight 12,000 pounds
(5,400 kg)

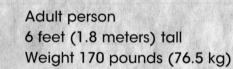

TABLE OF CONTENTS

WHAT'S INSIDE?

Armored dinosaurs! These animals lived in many places in the prehistoric world. Find out how they survived millions of years ago and what they have in common with today's animals.

ARMORED DINOSAURS

Dinosaurs lived between 230 million and 65 million years ago. Some dinosaurs were meat-eaters and some were plant-eaters. A few ate a mixture of meat and plants. The meat-eaters hunted the plant-eaters for food. To protect themselves, some of the plant-eaters grew armor on their bodies.

A baby *Pawpawsaurus* dropped its shoulders to stick out sharp spikes. It tried to scare away an attacker by showing body armor.

SCUTELLOSAURUS

Pronunciation:
skoo-TELL-o-SAW-rus

Scutellosaurus was a small dinosaur that lived in what is now North America. It had body armor on its back. The armor was made from lots of bony plates called scutes. If danger approached, this dinosaur could run away quickly. Its armor did not slow it down.

Body armor today

Some modern lizards have heavy scales, but they can still run from danger just as *Scutellosaurus* once did.

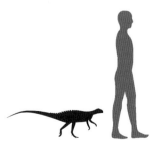

Size Comparison

6

Scutellosaurus was often chased by meat-eaters. But it was a fast runner and could often escape to safety.

SCELIDOSAURUS

Pronunciation:
skel-EYE-doe-SAW-rus

Scelidosaurus was covered in armored plates from head to tail. It was one of the first of the armored dinosaurs. It probably explored the beach, searching for plants along the seashore.

Foraging today

The modern warthog will eat just about anything. It sniffs at ground plants, just like *Scelidosaurus* did long ago.

Size Comparison

Scelidosaurus searched under stones along a beach, looking for tasty plants to eat.

GASTONIA

Pronunciation:
gas-TOE-nee-uh

What a fighter *Gastonia* was! Armor plates on its tail stuck out like knife blades. If it hit an attacker with its tail, the blades made deadly cuts. *Gastonia's* back and sides were covered in bony plates and spikes, protecting it from attackers.

Deadly tails today

A modern scorpion has a tail as deadly as *Gastonia's* was. The scorpion is armored as well, but it can also sting—something *Gastonia* was not able to do.

Size Comparison

Gastonia backed toward an attacking _Utahraptor_. If the meat-eater charged, _Gastonia_ swung its deadly tail into action.

PAWPAWSAURUS

Pronunciation:
PAH-pah-SAW-rus

Pawpawsaurus lived on open plains. Even though it often lowered its head to the ground to eat plants, this dinosaur did not worry about attacks. Its back was covered in armor for protection. Even its eyelids had armor on them!

Low grazers today

The modern bison eats with its head close to the ground. It doesn't have armor like *Pawpawsaurus* once did, but horns protect it from attacks.

Size Comparison

12

Pawpawsaurus ate ferns that grew close to the ground. It was a heavy animal and was probably a slow mover.

STRUTHIOSAURUS

Pronunciation:
STROO-thee-o-SAW-rus

Struthiosaurus was a small armored dinosaur. It had bony spikes on the neck and armor along the back and tail. It ate any plants it could find. Fossils of this dinosaur have been found on small islands in Europe. There may not have been much food on its island home.

Island feeders today

The modern land iguana lives on the Galapagos Islands, off the western coast of South America. It eats ground plants, as *Struthiosaurus* once did.

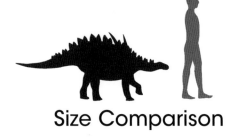

Size Comparison

Struthiosaurus fed along the shoreline. Body armor protected it from the fierce seabirds that also lived there.

ANKYLOSAURUS

Pronunciation:
ANG-ki-lo-SAW-us

Ankylosaurus was the biggest and heaviest of the armored dinosaurs. It had armor on its eyelids and a huge, bony club on the end of its tail. With a swing of this club, *Ankylosaurus* could scare, injure, or kill an attacker.

Armor today

The most fully-armored animal today is the armadillo. However, the modern armadillo is not nearly as big as *Ankylosaurus* was.

Size Comparison

When attacked by a meat-eater, *Ankylosaurus* swung its clubbed tail. Attackers usually backed away before getting hurt.

17

AMPELOSAURUS

Pronunciation:
AM-pel-o-SAW-rus

Not all armored dinosaurs were short, stout animals. A few, such as *Ampelosaurus,* were tall, with long legs and a long neck. *Ampelosaurus'* back was covered in bony plates and spikes that grew through its thick skin. This armor may have helped support the dinosaur's weight.

Big animals today

Although today's elephants don't have long necks as *Ampelosaurus* once did, they can reach up high with their trunks.

Size Comparison

A small herd of
Ampelosaurus moved
across a muddy plain,
eating along the way.

19

MAGYAROSAURUS

Magyarosaurus was the smallest of the long-necked armored dinosaurs. It had many bony plates on its back. The plates were set flat against the skin. This dinosaur ate low plants and leaves high in trees. *Magyarosaurus* lived on islands at the very end of the age of dinosaurs.

Armored leaf-eaters today

The modern Indian rhinoceros' skin is thick and coarse, like the body armor of *Magyarosaurus* was.

Size Comparison

On its island home, an armored *Magyarosaurus* stripped leaves from trees along the coast.

21

Where Did They Go?

Dinosaurs are extinct, which means that none of them are alive today. Scientists study rocks and fossils to find clues about what happened to dinosaurs.

People have different explanations about what happened. Some people think a huge asteroid that hit Earth caused all sorts of climate changes, which caused the dinosaurs to die. Others think volcanic eruptions caused the climate change and that killed the dinosaurs. No one knows for sure what happened to all of the dinosaurs.

GLOSSARY

armor—a protective covering of plates, horns, spikes, or clubs used for fighting

ferns—plants with finely divided leaves known as fronds; ferns are common in damp woods and along rivers

herd—a large group of animals that moves, feeds, and sleeps together

plain—large area of flat land with few large plants

plates—large, flat, usually tough structures on the body

scutes—pieces of bony armor set into the skin of a dinosaur

spike—a sharp, pointed growth

TO LEARN MORE

MORE BOOKS TO READ

Clark, Neil, and William Lindsay. *1001 Facts About Dinosaurs.* New York: Dorling Kindersley, 2002.

Dixon, Dougal. *Dougal Dixon's Amazing Dinosaurs.* Honesdale, Penn.: Boyds Mills Press, 2007.

Holtz, Thomas R., and Michael Brett-Surman. *Jurassic Park Institute Dinosaur Field Guide.* New York: Random House, 2001.

ON THE WEB

FactHound offers a safe, fun way to find Web sites related to topics in this book. All of the sites on FactHound have been researched by our staff.

1. Visit *www.facthound.com*

2. Type in this special code: 1404840176

3. Click on the FETCH IT button.

Your trusty FactHound will fetch the best Web sites for you!

INDEX

LOOK FOR ALL OF THE BOOKS IN THE DINOSAUR FIND SERIES: